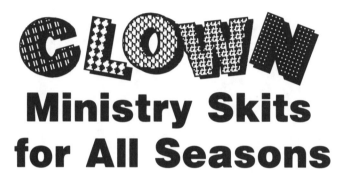

Ministry Skits
for All Seasons

By Floyd Shaffer

Loveland, Colorado

Clown Ministry Skits for All Seasons

Copyright © 1990 by Floyd Shaffer

Credits
Edited by Eugene C. Roehlkepartain
Designed by Jill Bendykowski
Cover design by Jill Bendykowski
Cover photo by Brenda Rundback
Illustrations by Ed Koehler

Library of Congress Cataloging-in-Publication Data
Shaffer, Floyd, 1930-
    Clown ministry skits for all seasons / by Floyd Shaffer.
        p.   cm.
    Includes index.
    ISBN 1-55945-053-3
    1. Clowns—Religious aspects—Christianity. 2. Drama in Christian education.
    I. Title.
    BV4235.C47S535   1990
    146'.7—dc20   90-46166
                                                                                         CIP

14 13 12 11 10 9   04 03 02 01 00 99
Printed in the United States of America.

Visit our Web site: www.grouppublishing.com

CONTENTS

100717

SKITS FOR MAJOR MILESTONES

ACKNOWLEDGMENTS

There's no way I could've created all the ideas in this book alone. When I set out to do this book, I remembered the many people who gave me ideas, support and the gift of all-around foolishness.

Many of those people were from Columbia, Maryland, where "clown ministry," from my perspective, was born. One group had its mission in the Kitamaqundi Community, a Christian community led by Dr. Gerald Goethe, a friend and "brother" for more than 25 years. We got together in the community's meeting place, an 18th-century carriage house, to brainstorm many of the ideas in this book.

I also say thank you to Ellen Barrick, Ann Baruah, Robert Berger, Mary Carrington, Peg Chester, Ann Davis, Jerry Dean, Grace Garrett, John Garrett, Gerald (Jerry) Goethe, Marge Goethe, Mary C. Goins, Ellen King, Gwendolyn Maples, George W. Martin, Ellery M. (Rick) Miller Jr., George Pappas, Ruby Racine, Ruth Smith and Arlene J. Trapp.

In addition, I thank Deb Laughery, whose word-processing skills made this manuscript possible. As a budding clown, she offered useful insights on these skit ideas.

INTRODUCTION

People love to celebrate! Whether it's Thanksgiving or Easter or April Fools' Day or birthdays or Spinning Wheels Day (late July), we thrive on opportunities to mark special occasions.

I wrote *Clown Ministry Skits for All Seasons* to add new ideas and approaches to your celebrations. This book is designed to give clowns dozens of ideas to enhance worship and celebration throughout the year.

Book Organization

Clown Ministry Skits for All Seasons has three parts:

1. Skits for the Church Year—These skits revolve around celebrations that are part of the traditional Christian calendar. They begin with Advent and continue through All Saints Day. Even churches that don't officially follow a liturgical calendar celebrate many of the days with special events.

2. Skits for Holidays—These skits, arranged by the calendar year, mark specific occasions we celebrate each year from New Year's Day to Thanksgiving.

3. Skits for Major Milestones—These skits don't fit particular days of the year, but they mark significant turning points in the lives of individuals and congregations. They're arranged in alphabetical order, from baptism to weddings.

In addition to the skits, the book includes a short introduction to and a list of "Word Ticklers" for each occasion. These are words I associate with the particular occasion. They help me create new skits and revise old ones. Use these "Word Tickler" lists to spark your creativity as you brainstorm clown skits for each occasion. Use them to help you think of ways to adapt skits I've written for your own situation. Or use the words to help you create your own skits.

Clowns in Worship

Most of the skits in this book are designed for congregational worship. While many congregations aren't accustomed to having a clown in the sanctuary, clowning can provide a rich, meaningful worship experience.

Here are several suggestions for making sure the experience is positive and uplifting.

● **Check your routine in advance.** Get approval from your pastor well in advance before doing a skit in worship. Make sure your message fits the theme for the day. It's powerful when the scripture that is read, is *seen*. The two senses are greater than the sum of their parts.

● **Create an environment for worship.** Put your ego in second place to the task of leading people into worship. If your main goal is performance perfection, you're putting self—not others—first. Clowns give themselves away to help an audience own what happens. This is also the task of a servant.

● **"Underwhelm," don't overwhelm.** Boisterous, raucous physical movements can be lots of fun to do, but they're not good for communicating messages to audiences. Over the years, I've discovered that the best way to communicate through a clown routine is to underwhelm.

Make your point with quiet pacing, not fast movement. Remember you're in a time of worship. Your worship leadership isn't an opportunity to celebrate *your* freedom as a clown but an invitation to people to celebrate their own freedom before God in response to your prompting.

● **Be sensitive to timing.** Some clowns rush a routine or skit, and later discover that people didn't understand it. Other clowns enjoy themselves so much that they forget time and try to milk a routine beyond its usefulness.

Timing can't be taught; it must be caught. The only advice I can give is to not get so caught up in what you're doing that you forget your purpose. Listen carefully to your inner rhythm, and get people's reactions afterward.

● **Use the "children's time" effectively.** Many congregations have a children's message. Most people are more receptive to clowning in this context at first.

● **Maintain mystery.** When you're in makeup, maintain your silence to create an aura of specialness. Leaving your character and speaking will destroy the special clown mystique.

● **Be aware of your visibility.** Most churches are built for listening—not watching. If you're in a place with poor visibility, use routines that communicate from the waist up. Make sure people can see what you do.

● **Don't push too hard.** Throughout scripture we see God working with people where they are—not where they ought to be. Use that same principle as you clown in worship. Don't try to push clown ministry on people, and understand when people don't see the benefit of your worship style. When people begin to understand that clowns in your congregation are not a novelty but a meaningful element in worship, they'll be more receptive to your presence and message.

Background Music

All the skits in this book are designed for silent clowning. These skits can be greatly enhanced with effective background music. What makes it effective? There's no simple formula or style. But use these suggestions to help you determine effective background music for your situation.

● **Define the routine's mood.** What effect do you want the routine to have on the audience? Once you've decided, pick appropriate music. I've done the same experience as a clown using classical music, ragtime and blues. I used the classical music with a group of church executives, and the ragtime at a family gathering. Both groups commented on "how well the music fit."

● **Don't try to time your clown actions to the music.** When you're familiar with your music, tuck it in the back of your mind. Then when a song is about to end, just punctuate it with your action. Folks will marvel at how well your routine fits the music. (If they only knew!) Of course, this advice doesn't apply if you have a specific dance portion in the program.

● **Use instrumental music.** I find instrumental music more conducive to clowning than vocal music, which can divert an audience from the mood you wish to create.

● **Draw from your own heritage.** Each Christian tradition prefers certain music. Instead of breaking that tradition, build on that tradition to help people experience their own music in a refreshing, new way.

● **Use adequate sound equipment.** I've seen many fine clown programs lose their impact because of inadequate sound equipment. You don't need the most expensive, state-of-the-art equipment, but do use equipment that's adequate for the sanctuary or performance space. An investment in a compact but reasonably good sound system saves many headaches.

Co-Authorship

A talk show host once asked me, "How do you feel about people who use your routines?"

I didn't even need to hesitate: "Did they do a good job?"

Clowns have always shared ideas openly with others with the childlike trust that an idea will be used appropriately—in a fresh and new way.

In that spirit, none of the skits here is really complete. You'll find no finished scripts or instant routines. But you'll find lots of ideas to stimulate your imagination.

Pause as you read the skits. Add your own thoughts. Then allow your thoughts to help you transform the skits to your own situation. We're transformers; we're called to create moments when people are open to the Spirit who transforms each of us.

You may read a skit and respond: "I wouldn't do it that way. I'd do it this way ..." Or as you look at the modest list of celebrations I've included, you may ask, "Why wasn't such-and-such day included?"

If either response happens, I'm delighted. For you'll then join me in the role of a co-author.

SKITS FOR THE

CHURCH YEAR

While the secular world counts down the shopping days to Christmas, many Christians prepare to celebrate Christ's birth through the Advent season. The season, which marks the beginning of the church year, begins on the Sunday nearest November 30 in Western churches. Eastern Orthodox churches begin celebrating it on November 14.

PREPARING FOR THE LIGHT

Overview—Clowns clean the sanctuary to symbolize preparing ourselves for Christ's coming. They light the candle of hope in the Advent wreath. Use this skit on the first Sunday of Advent.

The Skit (For one or more clowns)

Before the worship service, put scattered papers, an upset wastebasket and a candle from an Advent wreath at the front of your worship space.

Begin playing (or have someone perform) the song "Prepare Ye" from *Godspell*. Enter the sanctuary and discover the rubble. Quickly put papers in the wastebasket, and lay the candle aside. Use brooms, feather dusters and other cleaning implements to give the area an enthusiastic but reverent cleaning. Take trash and cleaning tools out of the room.

Then rediscover the candle. Pull out a box of giant matches that you've soaked in water. Try unsuccessfully to light the candle. Then search for the unsoaked matches that you've placed in the pulpit Bible.

· Strike a match and light the candle. Place the candle in the Advent wreath. Celebrate the lighting with quiet joy, and leave as the song ends.

BREATH OF FRESH AIR

Overview—Advent is a time of newness. This skit symbolizes that newness by having clowns "welcome" fresh air into the room.

The Skit (For two or more clowns)

Enter the room and mime various respiratory problems—coughs, gasps of air, difficulty in breathing. Then have one clown pull out a small Bible and show it to other clowns, who read it together.

Then an idea hits you. Open a window. Ventilate the room with fans, hands and maybe an electric fan. Act delighted and refreshed. Encourage others to take a fresh breath—even the minister.

REATE THE JESSE TREE

Overview—Circus clowns occasionally do "running gags" that involve making multiple entrances until the gag is complete. Spread this running skit over the four Sundays of Advent. It uses a Jesse Tree—a bare branch you decorate each Sunday of Advent. The name is derived from David's father and the pictorial description of Jesus as a "root out of Jesse" (Isaiah 11:10).

The Skit (For two or more clowns)

On the first Sunday of Advent, enter the sanctuary near the begin-ning of worship, during music. Mount a large barren branch near the front of the sanctuary where it can stay for the four Sundays. Then during the offering, have clowns bring seven gifts to hang near the bottom of the branch as decorations. These gifts could be Christmas cards from a previous year hung with yarn. Leave the sanctuary reverently.

For the next two Sundays, enter during each offering time, and hang seven more decorations—each time placing the decorations above the ones you hung the previous week, thus gradually filling the tree.

On the fourth Sunday, complete the running skit by placing a star at the top of the branch. Have one clown carry the tree down the aisle out of the sanctuary, while others follow the star.

HE END AND THE BEGINNING

Overview—Each week, a clown carries a cross into the sanctuary. On the fourth Sunday, the clown forms the crosses into a manger. This running skit seems puzzling until week four, so don't explain it to anyone.

The Skit (For one or more clowns)

You'll need eight boards for this running skit. Four of them should be about 2 feet long, and four about 3 feet long—all about 6 to 7 inches wide. Make four crosses, using duct tape to lash pieces together. Fold the end of the tape under for a "handle" to unwrap the tape at the proper time.

On each of the first three Sundays of Advent, carry one cross down the aisle and place it in a visible location. Then quietly leave.

On week four, carry in the last cross as you did the previous weeks. Then later in the service, reappear. Take the crosses apart. Use the tape to put the boards together as a manger (see diagram). The four short pieces provide the two ends, and the longer boards form the manger itself.

Set the manger in a central location, and gently fill it with straw. Place a plain cloth on top, opened in readiness to receive the Christ-child. Leave the sanctuary.

WORD TICKLERS

Use these words to spark your own creativity as you adapt these skits—or create your own—for Advent. Add other words you associate with the season.

- Advent calendar
- Advent wreath
- anticipation
- busyness
- candles
- cleansing
- coming
- decorations
- evergreens
- four weeks
- hope
- Jesse Tree
- John the Baptist
- love
- new church year
- preparation
- purple or blue
- quietness
- shopping
- straight path
- waiting

CHRISTMAS

The Nativity of Jesus Christ has historically been celebrated for 12 days. But most people focus on Christmas Day, December 25. We stand in awe as we celebrate how the glory of God was revealed in the rubble of life—through the gift of Jesus Christ.

TO THE LEAST OF THESE

Overview—It may seem strange to deal with homelessness and loneliness at Christmas, but both are very much a part of Jesus' birth. This quiet and poignant skit demonstrates the caring and sharing among those who have so little, as two tramp clowns celebrate Christmas together.

The Skit (For two "tramp" or "hobo" clowns)

Have a refrigerator box lying open at the front of the room so people can see in it. As quiet music plays, Clown One slowly enters the room, carrying a tattered bag and a toy pet on a leash of tattered rope.

Clown One goes to the box, sets down the bag, lovingly pets the animal, then ties the leash to the box. Then the clown reaches into the box and pulls out a small sardine can with one last morsel. (Use a large candy fish, or make something from a cold cut.) As the clown is about to eat it, he or she notices the animal. The clown starts to eat the morsel several times, but finally lovingly gives it to the pet.

Next, Clown One pulls a tattered stocking from the bag and hangs it on the box entrance. He or she also pulls out other decorations, such as a broken evergreen branch and a crude paper chain, and hangs them as decorations. Finally, the clown pulls out a small, tattered blanket, crawls into the box, covers him- or herself with the blanket, cuddles the animal and falls asleep.

Then Clown Two enters, also carrying a worn bag. This hobo looks in box, sees the pet and picks up the empty sardine can. He or she takes a can or box of pet food from the bag, makes a bow from yarn to wrap the food and sets it down. Clown Two also pulls out a somewhat better stocking and replaces the one that's hanging on the box. Finally, he or she folds the bag and puts it away.

Clown One awakes with a start and sees Clown Two shivering. Clown One also discovers the new stocking and pet food. With slow thoughtful looks, Clown One places the tattered blanket around Clown Two's shoulders. Then holding the pet, the two clowns quietly leave together.

SURPRISING GIFT

Overview—Many congregations celebrate communion
at Christmas. This skit illustrates the surprise we find in God's gifts as the clown discovers the communion elements in a manger.

The Skit (For one clown)

Enter the sanctuary, carrying a manger with a large red ribbon and bow around it. Make sure the straw is visible, and a small blanket covers it. Place the manger conspicuously in the front. Exit.

After the regular offering, enter again, untie the ribbon and gently remove the communion elements, which are hidden under the blanket. Place the communion elements on the altar or communion table. Pause reverently for a moment, and then leave as the communion service proceeds.

E ARE ALL GIFTS

Overview—Giving is an important part of Christmas. This skit reminds us that the greatest gift we can offer is ourselves, as one clown who doesn't have a gift helps others see they are gifts.

The Skit (For three or more clowns)

All clowns enter the room, each carrying a colorfully wrapped gift box with a large bow on it. One clown has no gift, just a bag. As other clowns place gifts on the altar with delight, the giftless clown stands forlornly to the side.

While the others stand watching the giftless clown in low-key disgust, the giftless clown takes a stick-on bow from a bag, attaches it to his or her shoulder or hat, and kneels. Other clowns understand. Then the single clown takes bows from the bag and sticks one on each of the other clowns, who all kneel.

All clowns leave, putting bows on the ministers and others in the congregation. If possible, give a bow to each worshiper.

WORD TICKLERS

Use these words to spark your own creativity as you adapt these skits—or create your own—for Christmas. Add other words you associate with the season.

- angels
- babies
- birth
- candlelight
- caroling
- Christ-child
- consumerism
- excitement

- gift
- giving
- God with us
- homelessness
- incarnation
- Jesus
- joy
- music

- peace
- presents
- Santa Claus
- Scrooge
- shepherds
- singing
- stars
- tree

E piphany—also called the Feast of the Three Kings—isn't one of the most familiar Christian celebrations in North America, though it's widely celebrated in Europe and Latin America.

In Western churches, Epiphany commemorates the Magi or Wise Men who brought gifts to the baby Jesus. It focuses on the manifestation of the Christ for all people, and its symbol is the star. (Eastern churches mark Jesus' baptism on this day.) It takes place on January 6, though it's usually celebrated the first Sunday of January.

GIFTS FROM WISE CLOWNS

Overview—Just as the Wise Men brought gifts to the Christ-child, this skit reminds us each to bring God our gifts—our time, talents and treasures. Use this skit before the day's scripture reading.

The Skit (For four or more clowns)

With background music playing, such as "We Three Kings of Orient Are," have one clown walk down the aisle carrying a long pole with a star hanging from it.

Not far behind, have three clowns follow, searching and being led by the star. Go to the front of the sanctuary where a manger sits. Then each clown presents one of the following gifts:

1. An oversize clock, symbolizing time;

2. A huge hammer or wrench, symbolizing talents; or

3. A giant credit card, symbolizing treasures.

Then pull back the blanket on the manger and find a Bible. Hand the Bible to the minister or worship leader, and leave. Then have the minister or leader read the scripture.

▓LET YOUR LIGHT SHINE

Overview—Epiphany celebrates a time of reaching out to people with the good news of God's love. This skit symbolizes this theme as clowns create a merry-go-round of candlelight.

The Skit (For three or more clowns)

You'll need a *large* candle with small rolls of crepe paper attached to the base or holder. Each clown also needs a simulated candle, made by rolling paper into a tube to fit over the index finger, then attaching an orange flame to the top. Place the simulated candles where the clowns can pick them up when needed.

For best effect, dim the lights. Enter the room with all clowns showing off different kinds of lights—a camera flash, a small flashlight, a lamp with a small bulb, an "atomic bulb" (a bulb that lights by itself) from a magic store, matches or a Cyalume glow stick.

One clown holds the large candle and lights the candle using another candle or a book of matches. Others make fun of the candle, but the clown holds the candle high. Then he or she discovers the rolls of crepe paper, and invites each clown to take one, roll it out and create a merry-go-round.

Clowns each put a candle tube on their index finger. Have the congregation start singing "This Little Light of Mine." Invite people each to raise their index finger as they sing. Clowns move in a slow merry-go-round circle throughout the song. At the end of the song, the clowns place the large candle on a small table and leave with the candle tubes.

STAR SEARCH

Overview—The star that directed the wise men to the Christ-child has become an important symbol for the "quest." We look for the star to guide us, and often find God has made us each a "star."

The Skit (For five or more clowns)

Decorate a wild poster with the words "STAR SEARCH" colorfully printed on it. Have one clown come out with the poster, showing it as a TV host might do—with lots of bowing—and getting people to applaud.

Then other clowns come out, one at a time, each performing an act—miming a singing solo, playing a kazoo, juggling, making a balloon poodle, blowing bubbles or bubble gum, or whatever the clowns do. The host exaggerates pleasure and milks applause.

Then the last clown comes out and simply stands, folds hands and bows his or her head. The host and other clowns grimace with embarrassment or hide laughter behind their hands.

When the last clown senses rejection, he or she walks to one side of the altar and grabs a fish line which goes across the altar (use small screw eyes to guide it). The clown pulls the line to raise a large star, which has been concealed. Then the clown walks over to where the star was and finds a box of stick-on stars. He or she gives one to each clown. Each celebrates being a star. If you wish, distribute stars to everyone in the congregation.

WORD TICKLERS

Use these words to spark your own creativity as you adapt these skits—or create your own—for Epiphany. Add other words you associate with the season.

- all people
- appearance
- arise
- boldness
- camels
- candlestick
- evangelism
- fireworks
- following
- generosity
- gifts
- glory
- incense
- Morning Star
- searching
- shine
- stars
- Wise Men

ASH WEDNESDAY

A sh Wednesday marks the beginning of Lent, a time of repentance before Easter. Traditionally, it involves spiritual preparation
and a call to repentance. The visual reminders of sackcloth and
ashes dramatize the reality of sin and the gift of God's forgiveness.

ASHES OF REPENTANCE

Overview—Clowns throw "sins" into a wastebasket where
the sins are burned. Then clowns use the ashes to draw crosses on
their hands and the hands of those in the congregation.

The Skit (For one or more clowns)

Make a small can of black ashes using small, charred pieces from
a fireplace or by burning last year's palm branches or small pieces
of heavy cardboard. Put the can of ashes in a metal wastebasket.

Get some flash paper and flash powder at a magic store. If
they're not available, use an inflated balloon with a bit of talcum
powder in it. Put the flash paper and flash powder (or the balloon)
next to the can of ashes in the wastebasket. Place the wastebasket at
the front of the room.

Enter the room. Unroll and display paper signs with sins written
on them, such as pride, greed and apathy. After displaying the signs,
wad them up tightly and put them in the wastebasket opposite the
ashes and can with flash paper and smoke powder.

When you've thrown away all the sins, light a wooden match and toss it *carefully* into the can with flash paper and smoke powder (or make sure the match pops the balloon to give a smoke-like puff).

Lift out the can of ashes and draw a cross on the back of each clown's hand. Have each clown take a small container of ashes and do the same for everyone in the congregation while music plays.

REND YOUR HEART

Overview—Joel 2:13 is a graphic call to authentic repentance: "Rend your hearts and not your garments." This skit picks up that theme as people tear paper hearts and receive new hearts.

The Skit (For one or more clowns)

Begin by silently passing a small paper heart (at least 2 inches across) to each worshiper. Have the minister lead a prayer of repentance or confession. Next, stand by the altar and tear a large heart halfway down. With appropriate gestures, invite the congregation to "rend their hearts" too. Then pass the offering plates to receive the torn hearts. Present the hearts as an offering.

Without the congregation seeing you, exchange the torn hearts for whole hearts. After the minister gives words of assurance, redistribute the offering plates and invite people to take a whole heart, God's gift.

WORD TICKLERS

Use these words to spark your own creativity as you adapt these skits—or create your own—for Ash Wednesday. Add other words you associate with the occasion.

- abstinence
- ashes
- fasting
- foot-washing
- post-Mardi Gras
- reflecting
- repentance
- smoke
- solemn

LENT

Lent commemorates the 40 days Jesus spent praying and fasting in the wilderness (Matthew 4:1-11). More than 1,500 years ago, Leo the Great described Lent as a time to prepare to commemorate Easter. It's a time for inner cleansing, for repentance of sins past, and for exercising love and reconciliation. Clowns can readily understand that Lent isn't a time for *not* doing things but a time for doing things intentionally.

It consists of the 40 days (excluding Sundays) before Easter.

FROM FEAR TO FAITH

Overview—Lent offers contrasts. This skit demonstrates that we can see things that look painful or negative through new eyes that make the things different.

The Skit (For one or more clowns)

Have a large box at the front of the room with the outside labeled "Danger," "Be Careful" and "At Your Own Risk." Approach the box and exaggerate reading the words. Mime fear by biting your fingers, shaking and slinking away. Start to open the box several times, then stop because of fear.

Finally, with great fear, lift the lid to release a helium-filled "love" balloon that's attached to a cross. (If no helium balloon is available, lift the balloon out.) With knowing looks, remove the balloon from the cross and gently offer the balloon to each clown, who holds it as you give a gentle hug.

Seeing the congregation, take the balloon to the front pew. Have people stand and receive the balloon with a hug. Go through the congregation hugging people. Then disappear.

 **HE UGLY CROSS**

Overview—Most modern crosses are pretty and decorative. But the cross Christians are asked to bear communicates pain and possible suffering. This skit contrasts different crosses as clowns make and distribute "ugly crosses."

The Skit (For three or more clowns)

Make kits for each person in the congregation that include a 6-inch branch, a 3-inch branch, a 12-inch piece of yarn and a 30-inch piece of yarn. Keep the kits together in envelopes.

Have clowns enter with several kinds of crosses. One can be gilded with gold paint, others with glitter, sequins or fuzzy material. Have clowns each hold their cross aloft, bow and place it on the altar or a table.

Then have another clown drag in a bedraggled, dead Christmas tree. The others silently mock. The clown trims and cuts the tree so just a trunk is left, then cuts the trunk in two and forms a cross using rope to tie the pieces together.

Place the cross upright near the box where you stored the envelopes. Have clowns each make an "ugly cross" using yarn and the branches from the Christmas tree. Have them each wear the cross around their neck.

Then have clowns distribute the envelopes to the people, who make their own crosses and put them around their necks.

SERVANTHOOD ISN'T AN OPTION

Overview—The towel of service is an important symbol for Christians, though we don't see it much. In this skit, only the clown who comes with a towel and a willingness to serve others can truly worship God.

The Skit (For three or more clowns)

Clowns enter with something that dirties their hands. For example, one might have a hot dog with mustard. Another might have a bucket of tempera paint. Another might have muddy coins. Each clown tries to kneel in reverence before the cross or altar. But none can bend their knees.

Then another clown comes in with a basin of water and a towel. He or she kneels, dips the towel in water and reverently washes the other clowns' hands. Now they can kneel!

The clown with the towel reverently holds it aloft, then places it on the altar or a table. Then clowns distribute precut "towels" (cut to about 2×6 inches) or disposable moist towelettes to everyone present so people can wipe each other's hands. The clowns then disappear.

WORD TICKLERS

Use these words to spark your own creativity as you adapt these skits—or create your own—for Lent. Add other words you associate with the season.

- abstinence
- basin
- cross
- daffodils
- deprivation
- desert
- faith
- fasting
- fear
- fish
- forty
- purifying
- reflection
- restrictions
- solemn
- spring
- suffering
- temptation
- towel
- water
- wondering

PALM SUNDAY

Palm Sunday is a paradox. Worship often begins on a joyful, happy note and concludes with silence to symbolize the entry into Holy Week in anticipation of Good Friday.

For the clown, this commemoration offers a chance to work at the feeling level, leading the congregation to the appropriate mood.

ASHES FROM PALMS

Overview—Since Palm Sunday offers a contrast of emotions, play off both happy and sad feelings. Clowns begin with joyful celebration, then discover the cross. The mood switches from celebration to reflection as they burn the palm branches.

The Skit (For one or more clowns)

Before the skit, put some ashes in a large metal container, such as a 3-pound coffee can.

Enter the sanctuary joyfully, waving palms and holding balloons. As you approach the front of the church, discover a cross. With awe and wonder, change your mood.

Begin tearing up the palm branches and place them in the metal container with ashes. Then set the palms on fire. When they've burned, stir the ashes with a wooden spoon. Pour out some ashes, and draw a cross in ashes on the back of each clown's hand.

Put ashes in small containers, and have worshipers draw crosses on each other's hand as the clowns disappear down the aisle.

A BALLOON'S CHANGING MOODS

Overview—This routine uses the running gag technique, communicating the message through a series of entrances when changes occur. Through the service, the clown's mood changes from joy to reflection as a balloon is deflated.

The Skit (For one clown)

Early in the service, enter the sanctuary with a very large balloon (try to find a 16-inch balloon that can be inflated to 20 inches) tied to a stick. Be joyful, celebratory and playful. Depart soon and quickly.

Then, at frequent intervals throughout the service, reappear, each time with the balloon deflated a bit. And each time, be less enthusiastic.

At the end of the service, enter the room with a completely deflated balloon. Slowly, dejectedly, walk down the aisle.

A SURPRISE IN THE PARADE

Overview—This skit captures the melancholy side of Palm Sunday, as the clown leaves a "love" balloon on the altar.

The Skit (For one clown—preferably a sad-face clown)

Come slowly down the center aisle at the beginning of worship, carrying a love balloon on a broken stick. Go to the front, take off your hat, bow and leave the love balloon on the altar. Pick up a small tattered palm on the floor, then exit down the center aisle.

WORD TICKLERS

Use these words to spark your own creativity as you adapt these skits—or create your own—for Palm Sunday. Add other words you associate with the occasion.

- balloons
- cheers
- children
- donkey
- flowers
- happiness
- jealousy
- joy
- new clothes
- palms
- parade
- paradox
- triumph

Maundy Thursday and Good Friday are somber times when Christians commemorate Jesus' sacrifice on the cross. The very nature of the observance may seem paradoxical for the presence of a clown—until we remember the clown's task is to present a clear and important message about God's love.

Y BODY, MY BLOOD

Overview—This routine is based on how I present the bread and cup for a communion service and can be done with or without communion. The clown visually shows how the bread and the cup are symbols of Christ's sacrifice on the cross.

The Skit (For one clown)

Enter the room with a box that looks like a gift. Open the box and take out a crude 2-foot-long cross. Set it on the altar or a table. Also take out a crown of thorns (about 8 to 10 inches in diameter made of real thorns, dried grapevine, or barbed wire) and place it on the cross.

Next, take out a loaf of bread and slowly and reverently place it beside the cross. Do the same with a communion cup.

Then hold up the cross in one hand and the bread in the other. Drop the crown of thorns over the top of the loaf, then slowly push the loaf onto the cross. Display it reverently.

Hold one-half of the bread, and vibrate the cross to break the loaf in half. Pause and show the broken parts. Then place the bread on the altar or table.

Take the cup or bottle in one hand and the cross in the other. Use three pouring motions, as if you were filling the cup from the arms of the cross. Shake the cross lightly to communicate emptiness.

With one hand holding the bottle or cup, use the other to gesture to it. Then slowly sweep your hand to the people in a "for you" gesture. Place the cup on the altar or table, and leave quickly and silently.

ISCOVERING THE CROSS

Overview—The clown sees the cross and pounds nails into it. Then each person receives a nail as a symbol of God's gift.

The Skit (For one clown)

Before the worship service, place a large wooden cross at the front of the room. It should be about 6 feet tall and made of crude limbs or lumber.

Enter the room during quiet music, carrying a hammer and a bag of nails. Discover the cross at the front and look at the hammer and bag of nails. Then slowly remove some nails, and pound them slowly and deliberately into the cross arms and the lower stem of the cross.

Next, walk to the offering plates. Hold the bag of nails aloft and pour them into the plate. With slow movements, beckon ushers forward to pass the plates. Encourage people each to take a nail. Then leave the room slowly.

EXTINGUISHED CANDLES

Overview—Many churches observe a Tenebrae service—a service of darkness—with the seven last words of Jesus as the focus. Each of the seven candles is extinguished as the words are read or commented upon. A clown can participate by extinguishing the candles.

The Skit (For one clown)

Enter slowly as the service begins, and light the seven candles. Stand nearby in the shadows. As each of the seven last words are read, extinguish a candle. When all seven candles are extinguished, walk out with a single candle as the minister concludes the service.

WORD TICKLERS

Use these words to spark your own creativity as you adapt these skits—or create your own—for Maundy Thursday or Good Friday. Add other words you associate with the observance.

- candles
- cross
- cross-carrying
- Crucifixion

- darkness
- death
- life
- lighting

- nails
- thieves
- thorns
- thunder

Throughout the church's history, Easter has been a time of great rejoicing and celebration. Jesus lives! Death is conquered! God's love is real!

Easter is a time to throw off the darkness and joyfully celebrate the light. I truly believe that laughter is the only authentic response to God's grace. What better opportunity is there for clowns to lead in worship!

THE TRANSFORMED CROSS

Overview—This skit might be appropriate at the beginning of worship. At first clowns are sad about the death as they look at the cross. Then they discover joy as the cross is turned to say, "He Is Risen!"

The Skit (For two or more clowns)

After the prelude, dim the church lights. Enter the church carrying a large 6- to 8-foot cross. On the side the congregation can see, have smeared paint streaks and nails to show its ugliness. *Keep this side toward the congregation.* Stand the cross at the front, and look at it with sadness, tears, fear, dejection and hopelessness.

Then have another clown enter joyfully, skipping down the aisle with an air of confidence. This clown goes to the cross and slowly turns it around. The reverse side of the cross has the words "He Is Risen" and is decorated colorfully with flowers and butterflies.

Bring the lights in the room up to full, and have the congregation join in joyfully singing the first hymn of the Easter service. During the hymn, mount the cross on a stand, dance around it and quickly disappear.

HE BUTTERFLY

Overview—The butterfly is a common Christian symbol of resurrection and new life. This skit uses liturgical or sacred dance to symbolize new birth at Easter as one clown is released from a paper cocoon.

The Skit (For one or more clowns)

Make a large cocoon using heavy construction paper (available at a lumber yard), or sew together two brown lycra dance bags (available from a dance supply store).

Pin large scarves to your wrists, armpits and waist to simulate butterfly wings. Then get inside the cocoon. During a prayer time, have other people or clowns drag the cocoon to the front of the sanctuary.

After the prayer, begin appropriate music such as "The Lord's Prayer" or a hymn. Break through the cocoon, stand and shed the cocoon. Then do sacred dance or choreography to the music.

AN EASTER SURPRISE

Overview—This skit is more of a giveaway than a routine. Clowns are sad that Easter is over, then another clown gives them eggs with crosses in them to symbolize the true gift of the season. Consider doing this on the Sunday after Easter to re-emphasize the day.

The Skit (For two or more clowns)

Collect enough plastic eggs for each person in the congregation. Make crosses from toothpicks, wooden stir sticks or tongue depressors to put inside each egg.

Enter the room carrying an Easter basket. Search through your basket, but only find empty candy wrappers, some eggshells and a couple of jelly beans. Express your sadness that Easter is over.

Then have another clown skip in with a basket filled with the plastic eggs. This clown gives other clowns each an egg and a hug. Open the eggs with great anticipation, and remove the cross. Then have all clowns join together to distribute eggs to the congregation.

WORD TICKLERS

Use these words to spark your own creativity as you adapt these skits—or create your own—for Easter. Add other words you associate with the celebration.

- bunnies
- butterflies
- celebration
- dawn
- eggs
- empty tomb
- excitement
- hats
- joy
- laughter
- life
- lilies
- morning
- new clothes
- new life
- Resurrection

Ascension Day is probably the least celebrated day in the Christian calendar. It marks the day Jesus was taken into heaven 40 days after Easter. On this day, Christians celebrate Jesus Christ's sovereignty as he has left our visible presence but remains Lord and King.

LIFT HIGH THE CROSS

Overview—Clowns release a cross that rises with "love" balloons. Then they share their joy with others by distributing cards that quote the Great Commission.

The Skit (For two or more clowns)

For each person present, make a small card that quotes Matthew 28:19a: "Therefore go and make disciples of all nations."

Then prepare a large cardboard box as follows (also see diagram):

1. Attach a lid to one side so it can be lifted easily.
2. Wrap the box in white paper. Tape red ribbon on the sides and

a large bow on top. Wrap it so you can flip back the lid without tearing the paper.

3. Cut a large cross from the thin white table covers most churches use. (Regular paper or other material won't work because it's too heavy.)

4. Use glue to attach lightweight sticks (such as balloon reeds) to the top of the cross arm, and to the top and bottom of the vertical portion. Overlap sticks, and tape them together to make a solid piece for the horizontal portion. *The cross must be lightweight.*

5. Tie several helium-filled balloons to the cross arms and top with light, strong thread. Attach a small weight, such as a button, to the bottom of the cross. Then carefully roll up the cross loosely from the bottom.

The number and size of balloons depends on the weight of the cross. In a large arena, I used a refrigerator box. The cross was 18 feet long, and I used seven, 16-inch "love" balloons. You can buy the mylar ones at gift stores, balloon shops or novelty stores. Many toy stores have helium, and some fast-food restaurants will let you fill your own balloons.

6. Put the balloons and rolled-up cross in the box, and close the lid.

The routine is simple. Enter the room carrying the box, and set it down. Mime anticipation and wonder. Then lift the lid to let the cross rise.

As you wave toward it in awe, have another clown look in the box and discover a small box with the cards. Read a card together. Then have one clown have an idea to pass cards to everyone. Distribute the cards, and disappear.

SURPRISE PARTY

Overview—When Jesus ascended, he left his disciples in a "waiting" mood. So they gathered—probably with food—and remembered the Upper Room experience. In this skit, clowns prepare snacks and invite the congregation to share in the food together.

The Skit (For two or more clowns)

Begin this skit at the conclusion of worship. Enter the sanctuary, and quickly set up a card table with decorations and food, such as cookies, popcorn, raw vegetables and punch. Put on party hats and prepare to celebrate.

Then notice the congregation and get a great idea. Quickly disperse by twos, and get card tables preset with snacks and punch. Put them in the center aisle, down front, and near the exits. When tables are ready, have the minister pronounce the benediction. Lead people to the tables, and act as silent servers. Have some appropriate music, either recorded or live as background for the party.

WORD TICKLERS

Use these words to spark your own creativity as you adapt these skits—or create your own—for Ascension Day. Add other words you associate with the occasion.

- crown
- disappear
- farewell
- glorious
- go and tell
- goodbye

- grace
- Great Commission
- joy
- king
- King of Kings
- Lord of Lords

- majesty
- power
- praise
- royal
- throne
- up

P entecost is the birthday of the Christian church. On this day, seven weeks after Easter, we commemorate the founding of the church as recorded in Acts 2. This festival goes unnoticed by the secular society. There are no cards or popular symbols. So we're free to create our own appropriate symbols.

 **MPOWERED**

Overview—When the Holy Spirit came upon the disciples, they were empowered to do things they couldn't do before and "tongues of fire" came on them (Acts 2:3-4). This skit re-creates that visual image and reminds people that God gives us power.

The Skit (For three or more clowns)

Make a 6-inch "tongue of fire" from orange or red posterboard for each clown. Staple elastic cord to each like a headband about 1 inch from the bottom of the flame, so it'll stand erect.

Have a "lead clown" enter and stand quietly as an observer. Then have other clowns each enter and try to do something they can't seem to do, such as juggle, make a balloon sculpture, play a kazoo or blow up a balloon. When all have tried, have the lead clown approach each one and put a tongue of fire on their heads. They each perform their impossible task.

Form a circle and joyfully dance for a few moments. Then quietly kneel in reverence and leave.

HEARING IN THEIR OWN LANGUAGE

Overview—Acts 2 describes how people from many nations heard God's Word in their own languages. This skit simulates how Christ brings together people who can't otherwise understand each other. Clowns begin by showing signs in foreign languages that no one understands. Then they turn the signs so everyone understands their love.

The Skit (For five or more clowns)

On sheets of posterboard, write "I love you" in foreign languages—one language per sheet. On the other side, write it in English. Here are some sample translations:

Chinese	Wo Ai Ni
French	Je T'aime
German	Ich Liebe Dich
Hebrew	Ani Ohev Otakh
Japanese	Watakushi-Wa Anata-Wo Aishimasu
Korean	Tangsinul Sarang Ha Yo
Spanish	Te Amo
Swahili	Nikupenda
Thai	Chan Rate Khun
Vietnamese	Toi Yeu Em

Have clowns enter the room, each carrying a sheet of posterboard with the foreign language showing. Clowns mingle, bump in to each other and show the posters, which no one else can understand. Then have a loud noise, such as a chord on the organ, a slamming door or even a firecracker, which causes all clowns to freeze momentarily.

Then have all clowns turn around their posters, so they can each read what the others have. Celebrate the recognition and hug each other. Then go hug members of the congregation as you show them your sign.

GIFTS OF THE SPIRIT

Overview—Based on 1 Corinthians 12:4-11, this skit shows how Pentecost bestowed gifts upon Jesus' followers. Clowns have a party and receive the "gifts of the spirit" in a box.

The Skit (For three or more clowns)

Clowns sit around a table as though they were having a party. They have everything they need—decorations, cake, party favors—except the presents. They look everywhere for the gifts.

Then another clown quietly enters with a large gift box. All the clowns rejoice and are eager to see what's inside. The clown opens the box and produces smaller boxes, each with a different gift of the Spirit written on the bottom, such as wisdom, knowledge, faith, healing, miracles, prophecy and tongues (or communication). Each clown receives a gift with a hug, and places the gift on the altar or communion table.

The clowns briefly kneel in prayer, then disappear.

WORD TICKLERS

Use these words to spark your own creativity as you adapt these skits—or create your own—for Pentecost. Add other words you associate with the festival.

- amazing
- birthday
- candles
- celebration
- empower
- energy
- fire
- flames
- healing
- Holy Spirit
- languages
- miracles
- power
- spirit
- wind

TRANSFIGURATION DAY

Transfiguration Day commemorates the time Jesus took Peter, James and John up a mountain where they saw Jesus as they'd never seen him before—as Son of God and Son of Man (Matthew 17:1-13). While they longed to maintain the "mountaintop" experience, Jesus took them back to reality where people laugh, cry, hurt and celebrate. Transfiguration Day is celebrated on August 6.

TRANSFORMED

Overview—In this skit, clowns discover a clown without costume or makeup. Transformation occurs as the other clowns make up and costume the new clown.

The Skit (For three or more clowns)

A person without makeup or costume enters quietly and sits on a chair, legs crossed and hand to chin to symbolize waiting. Clowns enter joyfully and playfully, and discover the potential clown. The person only looks bored.

Then one clown puts a red rubber nose on the person. Nothing happens. Other clowns try to figure out how to get the person to respond. Finally, they get an idea to make the person one of their own. Each clown has some part of clown makeup, and as the person sits quietly, the clowns apply the white-face makeup, then the red and accent marks. One clown produces a costume, perhaps a wig and hat, and the transformation is complete.

The clowns have their new friend stand, and show the new clown how to move arms and walk. With rejoicing and hugs, they skip out of the church together.

WORD TICKLERS

Use these words to spark your own creativity as you adapt this skit—or create your own—for Transfiguration Day. Add other words you associate with the celebration.

- action
- bright light
- changed
- eyes clouded
- glory
- honor
- sacred places
- transformed

ALL SAINTS DAY

The word "saint" conjures up strange images for some Christians. Yet the word itself simply means "one who believes." We all recognize those saints who walk through the pages of scripture—not as superpeople but as humans empowered by God.

Most traditions celebrate All Saints Day on November 1. Eastern Orthodox churches celebrate it on the first Sunday after Pentecost. Even churches that don't observe this day undoubtedly have times when they remember the faithful.

SURROUNDED BY SAINTS

Overview—In this skit, clowns are weighted down with mock weights. Then knowing they're surrounded by saints, they release their weights and celebrate freedom.

The Skit (For three or more clowns)

Make props to communicate heaviness by painting boxes black and using white paint to indicate various weights; for example 580 pounds or 200 pounds. Connect a piece of rope to each box.

On pieces of posterboard, write names of many saints. Include some from the Bible, familiar ones from history, some from your own tradition, some modern saints (Mother Teresa), as well as some faithful folk from your church—both dead and living.

Begin the skit by having clowns stumbling into the sanctuary dragging the weights behind them. Then have other clowns or helpers come out and surround them in a semicircle with the names of saints. Do this by hanging the signs on a line, taping them to various objects or asking people in the congregation to come hold the signs.

When all the saints are in place around the weighed-down clowns, have someone read aloud Hebrews 12:1. Have clowns each slowly and dramatically push the ropes from their shoulders. Then have them stand and demonstrate their new freedom in gentle movements. Finally, have each clown thank each saint with a handshake, hug, hand kiss, bow or whatever seems appropriate.

Then have all exit down the center aisle as the congregation sings an appropriate hymn, such as "For All the Saints."

WORD TICKLERS

Use these words to spark your own creativity as you adapt this skit—or create your own—for All Saints Day. Add other words you associate with the occasion.

● apostles	● dedicated	● life
● believers	● disciples	● martyrs
● called	● empowered	● prayerful
● committed	● faithful	● red
● congregation	● Holy Spirit	● remember

SKITS FOR

NEW YEAR'S EVE/DAY

People welcome a new year in different ways. On one extreme are those who hold raucous celebrations. On the other are those who see it as a thoughtful reminder that time steadily passes by in a relentless journey into the future. For Christians, the new year can remind us that our days belong to the Lord and that each day and each year is a gift from God.

FAITH THROUGH THE YEAR

Overview—In this skit, we see the old year recounting the past, and the new year offering an open future.

The Skit (For two or more clowns)

Make or purchase two calendars—one to represent the past year and one to represent the coming year. On each appropriate month of the *past* year, write the following:

- January—Hope
- February—Love
- March—Faith
- April—Joy
- May—Sharing
- June—Laughter
- July—Patience
- August—Prayer
- September—Caring
- October—Celebrating
- November—Action
- December—Praise

Have one clown represent the past year. This "Old Year Clown" should look older, walk with heaviness and be tired. Have a second clown represent the new year. This "New Year Clown" should act young and enthusiastic. Have a banner or sign around each clown's neck to indicate which year he or she represents. If you use more clowns, use signs or banners to identify which year they each represent.

Old Year Clown wearily enters and drops ungracefully in a chair. He or she holds up the past year's calendar so the audience can see it. The clown dozes.

New Year Clown romps into the room and awakens Old Year Clown by hopping, twirling and spinning with energy around the seated Old Year Clown.

New Year Clown then shows the new year calendar to Old Year Clown so the audience can see it too. New Year Clown flips through the empty calendar pages with pleasure and anticipation.

Old Year Clown patiently watches, then shows the old year calendar so the audience can see the words written on each month. The two clowns compare calendars.

Then the New Year Clown tucks the old year calendar into the new year calendar. The two clowns embrace and leave.

WORD TICKLERS

Use these words to spark your own creativity as you adapt this skit—or create your own—for New Year's Eve or Day. Add other words you associate with the celebration.

- aging
- anticipation
- beverages
- calendars
- change
- clocks
- confetti
- dreams
- fireworks
- food
- future
- history
- hopes
- memories
- parties
- plans
- resolutions
- time

MARTIN LUTHER KING JR.'S BIRTHDAY

What can we do to right a wrong? How can we turn people toward good? What can one person do?

Thank God that, through history, people such as Martin Luther King Jr. have shown that one person really can make a difference. A minister and a leader, King devoted his life to making his dream of "justice for all" come true. The United States honors his memory and his dream with a holiday on the third Monday of January, though his actual birthday is January 15.

EOPLE UNITED

Overview—Clowns plant "people seeds" that sprout in unity when air from a "love" balloon is blown on them.

The Skit (For one or more clowns)

Prepare the following props for the skit:

● Make 20 paper dolls—four each of red, black, white, brown and yellow, symbolizing the world's ethnic diversity. Attach 15 together by the hands to form a circle. Leave one different-color set of five unattached.

● Make three-dimensional "seeds" by cutting 30 seed-pod shapes using red, black, white, brown and yellow construction paper. Tape two together with something inside such as foam rubber chips or pieces of crumpled paper.

● Fold a sheet of posterboard in half and tape two sides to make a "seed envelope." In large letters, write "PEOPLE SEEDS" on one side. Draw a closing flap.

● Conceal an empty can in a large planter or other container, and gather planting tools such as a trowel, small shovel and sprinkling can. Place all the paper dolls in the planter, outside the empty can. Keep the unattached dolls separate from the others.

● Put a deflated love balloon in a Bible or another appropriate place.

Begin by entering and placing the planter in a central place. Carry in the gardening tools, accidently dropping them along the way. Show the "PEOPLE SEEDS" envelope to everyone, and gesture your intentions to plant the seeds. Pantomime working the soil and planting the seeds, making sure people see the different colors.

Then watch and wait expectantly. Nothing happens. Then have an idea, and produce the watering can. Pour water into the concealed container. Wait expectantly. Then with delight, pull out the five individual paper dolls. Express concern that they're all separated. With frustration, put the paper dolls back in the planter.

Next, discover the balloon in the Bible and blow it up. Make sure people see the word "love." Let the air out as you aim it into the planter. Or simply put the balloon into the planter. With delight, re-move the chain of multicolor paper dolls from the planter. Have several people hold up the dolls in a circle, and move in a circle.

I sometimes ask someone to hold a globe or a plastic ball of the world in the middle of the circle to show all people dancing hand in hand around the world.

WORD TICKLERS

Use these words to spark your own creativity as you adapt this skit—or create your own—for Martin Luther King Jr.'s Birthday. Add other words you associate with the celebration.

- busing
- civil disobedience
- civil rights
- equality
- "I have a dream"
- integration
- justice
- "Let freedom ring"
- marches
- Nobel Peace Prize
- non-violence
- opportunity
- peaceful confrontation
- personal worth
- racism
- respect

Valentine's Day, February 14, is a chance for people to express their love and affection for those around them. Often, messages are sent with a hint of mystery surrounding the sender. The day is a great time to affirm each other and to show love. It's also a good time to remember God's love.

 VALENTINE FROM GOD

Overview—Clowns unwrap a present from God to discover small crosses inside, which they distribute to the congregation.

The Skit (For two clowns)

Sit in a chair waiting impatiently. Show impatience by checking time on an alarm clock, looking at a calendar or watching a kitchen timer. When the alarm goes off or the kitchen timer rings, have another clown enter as a mail carrier or delivery person with a giant box. Sign for the box while the deliverer waits and watches expectantly. The delivery person can then leave, or stay and participate in the excitement.

Open the large box to discover a small box. Open it, and discover a third. Continue through several boxes until you find a small, wrapped gift box with a card that reads "From God."

Pantomime anticipation, delight and joy, and remove the wrapping to show a heart-shape candy box. Open the box and discover it's filled with paper crosses (available from Christian supply stores) with small red hearts attached to each (available from gift and card shops). Show the "From God" card again, and distribute crosses to everyone.

GIVE SOME LOVE AWAY

Overview—A clown stands rigidly until other clowns are close enough to hug. Then all clowns move through the congregation giving hugs.

The Skit (For three or more clowns)

Enter and stand stiffly with arms rigidly extended to your sides. Have each hand covered with a red heart, and a sign around your neck that says "I am a Valentine."

Have one other clown enter and carefully examine this "Valentine" clown. When the new clown finally stands close, hug him or her. The clown then moves away in delight, hugging himself or herself. Return to the rigid stance and repeat the action until all clowns have entered.

Then get the other clowns' attention and make sweeping gestures toward the congregation. The clowns move into the audience, give hugs and silently invite people to pass hugs to each other. The clowns quickly disappear while the hugging moves through the crowd.

WORD TICKLERS

Use these words to spark your own creativity as you adapt these skits—or create your own—for Valentine's Day. Add other words you associate with the occasion.

- candy
- cards
- Cupid
- flowers
- gifts
- hearts
- love
- red
- romance

April 1 is a day of the clown. On this day, we remember that the world isn't always the way it appears to be. Those who seem wise may look foolish, while those who seem foolish may look wise.

On April Fools' Day, clowns make fun of things we sometimes take too seriously. In the process, they remind us we're human and life is full of surprises. As Mark Twain wrote, "This is the day upon which we are reminded of what we are on the other three hundred and sixty four."

Like the April Fools' tradition, clowning reverses ideas to provide humor and to help us see ourselves and the world in a new way.

A FEAST OF FOOLS

Overview—Clowns sponsor a spaghetti dinner in which people don't pay for the food, but for eating utensils. Proceeds support a local hunger effort.

The Skit (For two or more clowns)

Plan a spaghetti dinner with a simple menu—perhaps after worship. Advertise this event, saying the food is free and "non-proceeds" go to a local hunger program.

On the day of the dinner, have clowns enter and pass the food-laden table. They discover—with much anxiety—that there are no eating utensils. Then have a clown enter with a poster that says "Forks for rent—$2" (or an appropriate amount). Let the clowns serve, rent flatware and announce the total amount of money received for local hunger efforts.

LAUGHTER CLINIC

Overview—April Fools' Day reminds us of the importance of laughter for good health. In this skit, a clown doctor checks people's "mental" health at a "laughter clinic." Use the skit in an informal setting where people can participate. Be prepared to work hard, but this routine is always well-received.

The Skit (For two clowns)

Create a small enclosed doctor's office with dividers. Put a stool and a table in the room. In large letters, attach the words "Laughter Clinic" to a divider, and put a table outside for a reception desk for a "nurse" clown.

Hang a poster on the office wall titled "Laughter Check." Under the title, list the tests to be conducted:

● Funny Bone Condition
● Laughing Test
● Hug Test

Have the nurse lead individuals one at a time into the doctor's office and seat them each on the stool. Start the examination using a toy stethoscope and listen intently to various bones—ankle, thumb, elbow—but hear no response. Then put the stethoscope to patient's head and break into gales of laughter. Shake the patient's hand in glee at the first test's success.

Point to a second poster on the wall that looks like an eye chart. It has the following in a vertical column:

HA

HEE

HO

TEE

Point to HA, and cup your ear to get the patient to say it. Then, point to HEE and the rest with the same actions. Now tap HA three or four times, encouraging the patient to repeat the word every time you tap. Repeat with the other words. Shake hands and celebrate—the patient passed!

Move to the hug test. Have the patient stand. Extend his or her arms, moving them forward. Bending an arm at the elbow to make sure they work. Then offer a big clown hug.

Finally, take an oversize prescription pad and write something like "Ten laughs and six hugs daily." Sign your clown name with a "Dr." in front of it.

Repeat the procedure with other patients, varying your routine a bit each time. Because you'll have a steady stream of patients, hang an "I'll be back at _____" sign on your office wall when you take a break. If you're doing the routine in front of an audience, stop after examining three or four patients.

WORD TICKLERS

Use these words to spark your own creativity as you adapt these skits—or create your own—for April Fools' Day. Add other words you associate with the celebration.

- bizarre
- foolish
- fun
- humbling
- jokes
- laughter
- playful
- reversed roles
- sneaky
- surprises
- tricks
- unpredictable

MOTHER'S DAY

On the second Sunday in May, we remember the gifts of our mothers, who played such important roles in who we are. We celebrate their love, patience and care.

WHEN YOU CARE ENOUGH TO SEND THE VERY BEST

Overview—A mother clown meets the needs of others, then collapses with exhaustion. Other clowns honor her with gifts.

The Skit (For three or more clowns)

A "mother" clown enters sweeping the floor, picking up items and dusting furniture. She's obviously tired. She carries a bag on her shoulder with an item for each "child" clown who comes to her.

Other clowns enter one at a time, and the mother clown meets their needs in various ways. Think of an idea for each clown. Use these as starters:

● One may need a chair to rest. So she gives hers.

● Just as she opens a sandwich to eat, a hungry clown approaches. So she tears off a piece for herself and gives away the rest.

● One has a hurt finger, so she puts on an oversize bandage.

● One clown enters crying, so she wipes tears with a large handkerchief—blowing the clown's nose in the process.

● Another enters sadly and receives a hug.

After all clowns have received symbols and actions of caring, the mother collapses in a chair. The other clowns huddle in a group, produce a small bouquet of flowers, give it to her with hugs and leave together.

A MOTHER'S "ROLES"

Overview—It's common to say a busy person wears many hats. That's the basis of this skit, which affirms the many roles today's mothers have. A "child" clown recounts all the hats his or her mother wears. The skit ends with corny clown humor.

The Skit (For two or more clowns)

You'll need a stand or tripod to hold posterboard. Gather or make hats to represent different roles moms have.

A very childlike clown skips out and puts a "Mother" poster on the stand. Then the "child" extends his or her hand in a sweeping motion to introduce the "mother" clown, who enters without a hat. The child puts up a second poster that boldly pronounces, "My Mom Wears Many Hats."

At this point, you can use the child alone or have others participate. One by one, have a child place a poster on the stand with the name of a role. Then the person puts a hat on the mother clown to represent that role and gives her another object to represent that role. The mother puts one hat on top of the next (if possible), and piles all the objects around her. Here are some ideas:

● Cook—Give her a chef's hat and a plate of fast food, a rubber chicken, cookies or cake.

● Chauffeur—Give her a chauffeur's hat and a toy car, and have her mimic driving.

● Referee—Give her an umpire's hat and a whistle, and have her stop a fight between two child clowns.

● Nurse—Give her a nurse's hat, and have her bandage a child clown's finger with a long strip of white cloth.

● Worker—Give her a hard hat and a toy shovel.

● Housekeeper—Give her an old-fashioned bonnet and a feather duster, and have her clean some furniture.

Then the child clown displays a final "The Roles of Motherhood" poster with a blank space after the word "roles." The mother looks at it, then uses a marker to cross out the word "roles" and write "rolls." From a hidden place she produces a bag of dinner rolls and passes out one to each child. The whole group leaves, happily eating rolls.

WORD TICKLERS

Use these words to spark your own creativity as you adapt these skits—or create your own—for Mother's Day. Add other words you associate with the celebration.

● caring	● giving	● overworked
● changing roles	● healing	● sacrifice
● comforting	● hugging	● supermoms
● drying tears	● listening	● supporting
● feeding	● love	

MEMORIAL DAY

M emorial Day is a rite of spring. Swimming pools are filled. Boats are put on lakes. Neighborhoods have picnics. Lawns are mowed and fertilized. Winter garbage is collected and removed.
   In the process, we forget the true purpose of this last Monday in May—to remember those who died for their country. Many people also honor others who've passed away.

LEST WE FORGET

Overview—Not all clown routines are funny. We seek to communicate the truth—in an off-beat way. In this routine, clowns pay respect to those who've passed away and give people each a string to tie around their fingers as reminders of the day's significance.

The Skit (For three or more clowns)
   All clowns enter with tombstones made of posterboard, braced so the tombstones stand up. Create a cemetery by placing the tomb-

stones in neat rows, bringing in plants and flowers, and attaching small flags to a few tombstones. Then have all clowns stand side by side and take off their hats in reverence.

One clown steps forward with a bag or box, and displays a sign that says "Lest we forget." The box is filled with bundles of string or yarn about 6 to 8 inches long. The clown ties a string around each clown's right-hand forefinger. Then all clowns move into the congregation and tie a string around each person's right-hand forefinger. Clowns disappear when every person has a string.

A medley of patriotic music in the background enhances this routine.

WORD TICKLERS

Use these words to spark your own creativity as you adapt this skit—or create your own—for Memorial Day. Add other words you associate with the occasion.

● barbecues
● cemeteries
● flags
● flowers
● gardens
● graves
● parades
● peace
● picnics
● sacrifice
● sadness
● soldiers
● summer
● veterans
● war

Dads. For many people, fathers have immeasurable impact on their lives. We're indebted to them for their love, concern, nurture, support and friendship.

On the third Sunday of June, we honor fathers for what they mean to us. The day challenges all fathers to show love, care, joy and warmth to their children.

■T'S WHAT'S INSIDE THAT COUNTS

Overview—A "father" clown brings home a paycheck and gives it to the "mother" clown. The check is cut up as expenses are added, leaving a heart to give to the family.

The Skit (For three or more clowns)

A father clown comes slowly on stage, carrying a lunch box or briefcase, and a very large envelope with "paycheck" printed on the side. A mother clown and some children greet him.

The mother beckons for the paycheck. It's removed and shown. The mother holds up posters to show basic budget items: "housing," "food," "medical expenses," "repairs," "rubber chickens," "balloons." The father folds the check in half and, as each item is requested, uses scissors to cut a piece from the doubled check. He gives each piece to the mother or children.

The father clown keeps cutting pieces until the mother and children have had all their needs met. All that's left is a sheet of paper, which, when unfolded, is a heart. The father offers it to the others, and each receives it with a hug. A group hug with the heart raised ends the skit.

THE PATIENT FATHER

Overview—Perhaps the most poignant portrait of what a father can be is painted in Luke 15:11-32, where Jesus tells the parable of the lost son—also known as the parable of the waiting father. This skit uses a similar theme to show a father's love and gifts to his children.

The Skit (For two clowns)

A "father" clown and a "child" clown enter together, with the father leading a bored and reluctant child. The father is carrying a suitcase that's decorated clown-style.

Father places the suitcase on a small table and opens it. It's filled with various clown props. He shows delight by clasping his hands, then throwing them upward with joy. The child looks in, yawns, rolls his or her eyes and sits down in complete disinterest.

The father then takes various props from the suitcase and tries to teach various clown "arts" to the child. These can include:

● blowing soap bubbles;
● balancing a long feather;
● making a balloon sculpture;
● squeezing a bicycle horn; or
● tight-rope walking on a piece of string lying on the floor.

Yet the child pays no attention.

Then the father blows up several round balloons. The child suddenly notices, gestures for the balloons and the suitcase, and then rudely takes them and walks down the aisle without a look back. The father stands, waving goodbye.

The father sits patiently, periodically turning calendar pages and crossing off each month with a large pencil. To communicate passing time, the father can also turn from the audience and put on a fake beard.

While the father is waiting, the child plays at the back of the room. First, he or she plays with the balloons until one breaks or loses air. When balloons are gone, the child looks in the suitcase and tries to do the other clown acts—but can't.

Each failure causes more stress and anxiety for the child, until the child is completely exasperated. Then, with a finger snap, the child has an idea to go back home. He or she closes the suitcase and starts back down the aisle. The aged father, using binoculars (perhaps made from large cardboard tubes) sees the child, hobbles with glee and greets his child with a big hug.

The child puts the suitcase on the table, opens it and hands his or her father one of the items previously ignored, such as soap bubbles. The child watches carefully as the father demonstrates. Then the child tries with success. The child gives the father a clown hug and blows more bubbles as the father closes the suitcase. The two exit arm in arm, trailing soap bubbles.

WORD TICKLERS

Use these words to spark your own creativity as you adapt these skits—or create your own—for Father's Day. Add other words you associate with the occasion.

- breadwinner
- cars
- changing roles
- concern
- decisions
- distant
- help
- love
- meetings
- paychecks
- provider
- sports
- support
- time
- tired
- vulnerability
- work

INDEPENDENCE DAY (USA)

Each year, U.S. citizens celebrate the country's independence with parades, picnics and fireworks on July 4. We treasure the freedom the day commemorates and celebrate great moments in our tradition and history. But Independence Day is also an opportunity to remember the responsibilities we as citizens have inherited with that freedom.

THE STATUE OF LIBERTY PLAY

Overview—This skit is a playful but serious look at the country's promises and responsibilities. Through the skit, clowns "disassemble" the words on the Statue of Liberty.

The Skit (For five or more clowns)

Make a 6- to 8-foot cardboard Statue of Liberty. Then attach small posters to the base of the statue where the audience can see them.

Like the real inscription, the words say: "Give me," "your tired," "your poor," "your huddled masses yearning to breathe free."

The skit begins with a smug, powerful clown marching in to guard the statue.

Exhausted clowns enter and try to lie near the statue. But the guard makes the clowns leave. As the tired clowns leave, they remove the "your tired" poster.

Poor clowns enter with empty pockets, ragged clothes, empty grocery bags and other symbols of poverty. They, too, are rejected, and they remove the "your poor" poster as they leave.

Another group of clowns enters communicating fear and oppression (perhaps have them handcuffed or chained together). They are rejected. As they leave, they remove the "your huddled masses yearning to breathe free" poster.

Finally, a swaggering, confident and cocky clown enters, with arms crossed over his or her chest to conceal a sign. Going directly to the statue, the clown looks at the last words, laughs and takes off the poster. Then the clown turns and reveals the sign on his or her chest that says "IRS." The clown chases away the guard by waving the "Give me" poster.

WORD TICKLERS

Use these words to spark your own creativity as you adapt this skit—or create your own—for Independence Day. Add other words you associate with the occasion.

- bands
- Declaration of Independence
- fireworks
- flags
- freedom
- hot dogs
- independence
- justice
- liberty
- parade
- patriotism
- picnic
- revolution
- stars and stripes

In the early 1900s, young men in my father's farming community would go to town, race their horses on Main Street and build a large bonfire to mark the end of summer on the first weekend of September. As they gathered round the fire, they'd throw their cheap straw hats into it. After straw hats were burned, they'd wear only the heavy-weight clothing of fall—no matter how warm the weather.

Americans still mark the end of summer with the Labor Day holiday. We have barbecues, picnics, baseball tournaments, parades and, of course, sales. But Labor Day also gives us a chance to celebrate work, employment and vocation.

While people in North America celebrate Labor Day on the first Monday of September, other people around the world honor workers with a holiday on May 1, May Day.

LOOK WHAT THE LORD GAVE US

Overview—Clowns place symbols of their talents on the altar and remember their skills are gifts from God. This skit fits nicely before the offering.

The Skit (For one or more clowns)

Have a table at the front of the congregation. Skirt it neatly with white paper. Write "Look What the Lord Gave Us" on the front of the skirt.

Gather a variety of props that represent work or talents of people in your congregation—typewriter, hammer and saw, pile of computer printouts, stethoscope, a spatula with a hamburger to flip, gardening tools, mop and briefcase. (Use children's toys if you wish.)

Each clown enters with one work prop, uses it in clownlike fashion and places it on the table.

When all the items have been presented, encircle them with red ribbon. Put a giant bow on top of the pile with ribbon hidden inside it. Then pull from the bow a long length of ribbon and attach it to your altar or a cross. Bow your heads reverently and then thrust your arms upward to pantomime joyful thanksgiving as you leave.

WORD TICKLERS

Use these words to spark your own creativity as you adapt this skit—or create your own—for Labor Day. Add other words you associate with the day.

- calling
- chores
- county fairs
- daily bread
- factories
- high tech
- jobs
- labor unions
- parades
- skills
- talent
- unemployment
- vocation
- wages
- work

THANKS-GIVING

The Earth is a magnificent storehouse offered to us by the Creator to use and enjoy. Yet we often abuse God's good gifts. Instead, we ought to give thanks each day and not take the gifts of people and things for granted.

Thanksgiving Day occurs on the last Thursday in November in the United States. Canadians celebrate it on the second Monday of October. Thanksgiving Day gives us a special opportunity to offer our gratitude to the one who is the source of all good things.

THE THANKSGIVING CONNECTION

Overview—Clowns discover various items in a cornucopia and realize the items are all gifts. Then clowns give themselves as gifts to God in thankfulness.

The Skit (For two or more clowns)

Find a large cornucopia, or draw one on cardboard and cut an opening to simulate a place from which things can come. Also get a card table with a cloth drop to conceal items beneath it.

Gather a variety of items to symbolize food, clothing, shelter, time, abilities and money. Use your imagination to give a clown perspective. For example, use a rubber chicken to symbolize food, or use oversize shoes or a humorous T-shirt for clothing. Include serious and humorous items.

Then attach one end of a crepe paper streamer to each item. Attach the other end to the opening of the cornucopia. Place each item under the table.

Begin the skit by entering to the music of "Come, Ye Thankful People, Come" or other appropriate music. Discover the cornucopia on a table. With curiosity, follow a streamer from the cornucopia to one of the items under the table. Bring the item forward, display it and use pantomime to communicate that it's a gift. Then place it on the table. Continue through all of the items, with different clowns discovering different items.

When all gifts are displayed (with streamers still attached to the cornucopia), have a puzzled clown look at the cornucopia (scratching head, chin in hand). Then, with a snap of the fingers and an "Aha!" expression, have the clown produce another streamer. Have the clown attach it to the cornucopia and then to a cross placed on the altar or a table. Have the clown get an offering plate, put it on the floor and gently sit in it with hands raised in thanks.

Have other clowns take turns sitting in the plate. Then put it by the cornucopia. Leave the room reverently.

HARING OUR BLESSINGS

Overview—Thanksgiving is a time for sharing because we've been given so much. In this skit, a clown shares popcorn with other clowns—and with the whole congregation.

The Skit (For three or more clowns)

Prepare enough sandwich bags full of popcorn for everyone in the congregation. Hide them in a large pot or bowl. Make pilgrim hats for each clown out of construction paper.

Several clowns enter wearing pilgrim hats and sit at a small table at the front of the room. They each mime hunger by rubbing their stomach.

One clown enters with an electric hot plate or popcorn popper, puts it on the table and plugs it in. (Note: A little preheating helps.) This clown produces some unpopped popcorn and puts it in a pan or popper. All the clowns wait expectantly as the popcorn pops.

When it's popped, the clown pours it into the large bowl or pot that's filled with bags of prepopped popcorn. The "pilgrim" clowns enjoy the popcorn together. They huddle together, obviously in an intense discussion with many looks toward the audience. Then they quickly disperse, passing the small bags of popcorn to everyone. Create a mood of sharing and caring.

WORD TICKLERS

Use these words to spark your own creativity as you adapt these skits—or create your own—for Thanksgiving. Add other words you associate with the celebration.

- abundance
- blessings
- corn
- cornucopia
- family
- family reunions
- food
- friends
- giving
- harvest
- hunger
- Native Americans
- pilgrims
- prayer
- turkey

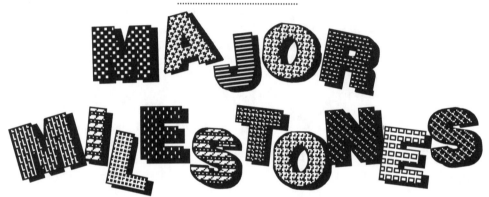

SKITS FOR

MAJOR MILESTONES

B aptism is an important occasion for Christians, marking their
becoming part of Christ's body, the church. Though practiced
many different ways, two elements are central: water and God's
Word.

Clowns can enhance such holy moments. Sometimes a simple
clown appearance can create a memory of baptism that words alone
can't.

OGETHER—WATER AND WORD

Overview—A clown symbolizes the spiritual significance of
the baptismal water by appearing to squeeze water from a Bible.

The Skit (For one clown)

Before using this skit, clear it with those involved in the baptism.

Enter in reverence and gentleness, carrying an easily recognizable
Bible. Inside the Bible, conceal a rubber squeeze bulb that holds
about a cup of water. (You can generally find these attached to
water-squirting toys in a novelty store or at a pharmacy. Or you can
use a kitchen baster.)

Slowly and reverently, raise the Bible over the font or baptistry.
Squeeze the Bible and produce a long-lasting stream of water. Leave
reverently.

WORD TICKLERS

Use these words to spark your own creativity as you adapt this skit—or create your own—for baptism. Add other words you associate with the occasion.

- adoption
- baptistry
- candles
- dove
- faith
- font
- Godparents
- Holy Spirit
- new life
- profession of faith
- rebirth
- shells
- sponsors
- water
- Word

The gift of life is one of awe, wonder and magnificence. Each year is an occasion for celebration. When someone wishes us a "Happy Birthday" through a card, telephone call or gift, we feel uplifted.

Clowns are often associated with birthday parties for children. But they're appropriate for birthdays for people of all ages. The clown's task is to create an environment for the celebration.

LET THEM EAT CAKE

Overview—Clowns "bake" a birthday cake using ingredients that help people grow. This routine can be used in worship to recognize everyone's birthday or at a group meeting around the birthday theme.

The Skit (For three or more clowns)

Find a large box that can hold a birthday cake, a large container and cake ingredients. Put a prebaked, decorated cake with candles on it in the box. Label cake-making ingredients with long strips of paper that you roll up and attach to each ingredient. For example, label the flour "God's love" and the sugar "parents." Label other ingredients "hope," "peace," "joy," "faith" or other words that help us grow and mature.

Put a table at a central spot. Have clowns enter wearing aprons or chef hats and carrying large spoons, mixing utensils, flour, sugar, eggs, milk, flavorings, cans of frosting and candles. Have another clown laboriously bring in the large box and set it on the table. Have another clown bring a large fake book labeled "Cake Recipe."

In typical fumbling clown fashion, have all clowns put the ingredients (the whole packages) into the large container in the box, showing the labels as they do it. After some stirring and commotion, pick up the box and carefully use a candle underneath to "bake" it.

Have all clowns peer in the box and show signs of delight as someone pulls out the real birthday cake with candles. Use the cake as the table centerpiece. Light the candles and have a non-clown lead the group in singing: "Happy birthday to us, happy birthday to us, happy birthday everybody, may God bless us."

Have other cakes ready, and share in an all-church birthday party.

A SPECIAL BIRTHDAY CARD

Overview—Clowns form a giant birthday card and visit people celebrating birthdays.

The Skit (For four or more clowns)

Make a giant birthday card from an old sheet or other white cloth. Keep the message simple, and decorate it with balloons, flowers or cartoon characters. Write a simple message such as "We wish you a happy birthday." Make neat holes in the cloth several clowns can put their heads through.

Visit someone to celebrate his or her birthday. Don't forget the elderly and homebound people as you do this. Check your church records for birthdays.

Have two clowns hold up the cloth while others put their heads through the holes. Ring the doorbell and, when the person answers, sing "Happy Birthday" (forget the silence this once). Give the person a balloon and a hug. Then leave—unless a party is in progress that you can add joy to.

WORD TICKLERS

Use these words to spark your own creativity as you adapt these skits—or create your own—for birthdays. Add other words you associate with the celebrations.

- aging
- cakes
- calendars
- candles
- cards
- decorations
- games
- gifts
- growth
- ice cream
- party hats
- songs

DRIVER'S LICENSE

G etting a driver's license is a rite of passage to adulthood for most teenagers. With a car, a teenager is no longer limited to how far can be traveled by foot or bicycle—or by a parent's willingness to be a chauffeur.

It seems appropriate that churches recognize this passage and all it symbolizes. Whether in Sunday school, worship, at a group meeting or surprise visit to the home, clowns might influence new drivers to be responsible behind the wheel.

THE RESPONSIBLE DRIVERS CLUB

Overview—Clowns take new drivers through a "test" and then initiate them into the "Responsible Drivers Club."

The Skit (For three or more clowns)

Choose a name such as the RDC (Responsible Drivers Club) or

ICDL (I Can Drive at Last!) or some name of your choice. Make "traffic" signs from yellow posterboard with words such as "Think," "Smile," "Wave," "Look," "Go" and "Slow Down."

Have a clown ride a tricycle to the front of your meeting area. Then have other clowns hold up different signs for the clown to follow. Have an "inspector" clown check off each one as the sign is obeyed.

Then invite the new "licensees" to take the tricycle test. When they pass the test (we hope!), have all clowns celebrate. Then give each person (and the riding clown) a poster-size certificate with gold seals and ribbons signifying membership in your driving club.

As a finale, have one clown display a sign that says "We give you a new car." Present a toy car with a ribbon on it, and a big key cut from posterboard with RDC (or your own club) printed across it.

WORD TICKLERS

Use these words to spark your own creativity as you adapt this skit—or create your own—to celebrate getting a drivers license. Add other words you associate with the milestone.

- adulthood
- courtesy
- cruising
- freedom
- independence
- insurance
- laws
- racing
- responsibility
- safety
- speed
- speed limits
- tests
- transportation
- wheels

FIRST DAY OF SCHOOL

The first day of school can be exciting and scary for children. Many have been looking forward to the day for a long time. But whether they're entering first grade, going to a new school or facing a new schedule, kids face new rules, customs, faces, expectations and routines.

By recognizing this important transition, a church can remind young people that they're important and that the church and God care about them.

I'M A VERY IMPORTANT PERSON

Overview—Clowns go to school, and one has trouble writing. The teacher helps, and all clowns are recognized as "Very Important People."

The Skit (For four or more clowns)

Write simple words such as cat, dog, boy and girl on a chalkboard, and put it at the front of the room. Have clowns sit in a row of little chairs or desks holding oversize pencils and small notebooks. Then have a "teacher" clown point to various words as "student" clowns write in their notebooks.

Have one clown (clearly visible to all) try unsuccessfully to write with the wrong end of a huge pencil (you can find these at souvenir shops). Have the teacher s-l-o-w-l-y turn the pencil around so the student can write properly—with great joy.

Next, have the teacher write "V.I.P." on the chalkboard with "Very Important Person" under it. Then have the teacher give a sticker or button that says "V.I.P." to each clown with a hug.

Have clowns go to children who are entering school to give each one a hug and a sticker or button.

WORD TICKLERS

Use these words to spark your own creativity as you adapt this skit—or create your own—to mark the first day of school. Add other words you associate with the occasion.

- apples
- books
- chalkboards
- crafts
- eagerness
- excitement
- fear
- friends
- grades
- ideas
- paper
- pencils
- principal
- reading
- school lunches
- studying
- teachers
- words

W hether people are graduating from kindergarten or graduate school, graduation is a significant milestone. Graduates have worked hard and completed an assignment. It's a transition churches often recognize. Clowns can add a special, fun touch to the event.

 ONGRATULATIONS!
YOU MADE IT!

Overview—Clowns honor each graduate with a mortar board, a giant "diploma," an award and a gift. Adapt the skit for use with the congregation, youth group or a surprise visit to the graduate's home.

The Skit (For one or more clowns)

Do the following in advance:

● Make cardboard mortar boards using the school colors for each graduate. Attach a small tab of paper to the top to simulate the tassel.

● In large letters, write a personal message to each graduate from the congregation on poster-size paper. Roll up the diploma and tie it with a school-colors ribbon.

● Create award ribbons, using blue ribbon and circular badges that have such honors as "#1 Person," "Very Important Graduate" and "First in Friendship."

● Wrap novelty gifts such as toy watches, a small teddy bear with mortar board or a jar of bubble-blowing liquid for each graduate.

Have graduates each come forward. (If you have a recording, play "Pomp and Circumstance.") Give graduates each a mortar board. With great flourishes, give graduates each a diploma, and let them open and read it (maybe even aloud). Then give graduates each an award ribbon with a suitable clown-style handshake. Finally, present the novelty gifts and wait while they're opened and demonstrated.

THE AWARDS CEREMONY

Overview—"Graduating" clowns receive awards, then other graduates are recognized with awards.

The Skit (For three or more clowns.)

Clown One enters, postures him- or herself, and plays "Pomp and Circumstance" on a kazoo. Other clowns wearing tiny mortar boards enter in fumbling steps and take seats facing the audience.

Clown One then holds up a poster that says "Awards Time." Have poster-size certificates with different awards on them, and have each graduating clown receive the award appropriately. Here are some ideas:

● Best Smile—Clown comes forward making exaggerated smiles.

● Most Athletic—Clown comes forward tossing—and dropping— a ball.

● Best Dancer—Clown does a crazy dance and trips over his or her feet.

● Best Musician—Clown plays a children's song on a kazoo or comb with tissue paper.

● Most Intelligent—Clown comes forward reading an upside-down comic book.

When all clowns have received their awards, they have a great idea. They bring forward all the graduates and have them face the congregation.

Then Clown One holds up a giant certificate that says, "U R Speshal Award" as all clowns mime celebration. Then the clown hangs a smaller version of the award that says "I M Speshal" around each graduate's neck. Clowns celebrate as the congregation applauds. The clowns disappear.

WORD TICKLERS

Use these words to spark your own creativity as you adapt this skit—or create your own—for graduation. Add other words you associate with the celebration.

- awards
- commencement
- congratulations
- diploma
- goodbye
- grades
- honors
- mortar boards
- parties
- photographs
- "Pomp and Circumstance"
- receptions
- robes
- speeches
- yearbooks

NEW CHURCH STAFF MEMBER

The arrival of a new pastor or other staff person in a congregation is a time of much anticipation and celebration. The installation service is generally shaped by denominational tradition. Yet the clown can often work within the structure to make the event unique. Or a clown can appear in an informal reception for the new church leader.

LET'S SERVE TOGETHER

Overview—Clowns present a towel of service to the new staff person and then give pieces of the towel to others in the congregation.

The Skit (For two or more clowns)

Make a large pillow heart using red cloth or felt. Stuff it so it's full but easily recognizable. You may wish to write "From the congregation" on it in white letters. Conceal the heart near the chest in one clown's costume that permits easy removal.

Have another clown carry a colorfully wrapped package that contains an old towel that can be easily cut.

At a predetermined time, "interrupt" the service and present the gift to the new staff member. After it's opened, drape it over the person's shoulder. Then, with great joy, have the first clown pull out the heart-shape pillow and present it to the staff person.

Gently wipe the staff person's hands with the towel. Then cut the towel into smaller pieces. Hand one piece to the staff person, and lead him or her to the congregation to gently wipe the hands of a person sitting along the aisle. Invite that person to wipe the hands of the next person as well as others seated nearby.

Give other pieces of the towel to others throughout the congregation. Clowns disappear as the hand-wiping continues until everyone is included.

WORD TICKLERS

Use these words to spark your own creativity as you adapt this skit—or create your own—for the arrival of a new pastor or other church staff member. Add other words you associate with the occasion.

- anticipation
- challenges
- criticism
- disappointment
- encouragement

- excitement
- expectations
- friendship
- hope
- ministry

- names
- new faces
- receptions
- servanthood
- unknown

Most people aren't excited about retiring (if they're honest). Some still feel productive, and wonder what they'll do now. Others worry about living on a limited income. Others aren't quite sure what they'll do after the first four weeks. But many people retire *to* something not just *from* something. They anticipate being active in new activities and interests.

Retirement offers clowns an opportunity not only to celebrate past accomplishments but also to celebrate the new possibilities of the future.

 **HE RETIREMENT PARTY**

Overview—Clowns invite the retiree to a party and give gifts to honor the transition.

The Skit (For three or more clowns)

Carry in a table and set it for a party. Quickly but clumsily set decorations in place. When all clowns are seated, notice an empty chair.

Have clowns each silently count themselves. Someone's missing. Then have an idea.

Go into the crowd and get the retiring person to join the party table. Give the person a clown hat and a red rubber nose. Pour some punch into the party glasses, and have one clown stand to give a toast. Have some clowns move their mouths and arms like they're talking and excited. Have others look bored and impatient. Then have one clown stand and gently make the toasting clown sit down.

Present envelopes or shallow gift boxes to the guest with various words printed on them. Find out some of the retiree's interests or hobbies, and make appropriate gifts. For example, one might say "free time" and contain a cardboard clock with the word "free" printed on it.

Next, present the last two gifts. One says "A Big Hug." Stand the person in the middle of a clown circle and embrace.

Then dismiss the retiree. As you do, have another clown run in with a big envelope that says "Your ticket to the future." Have the envelope contain an appropriate religious gift such as a prayer book, Bible, devotional booklet or a subscription to a Christian magazine.

WORD TICKLERS

Use these words to spark your own creativity as you adapt this skit—or create your own—for retirement. Add other words you associate with the milestone.

- boredom
- condominiums
- grandchildren
- hobbies
- interest
- Medicare
- Social Security
- time
- traveling
- uselessness
- volunteer
- wrinkles

WEDDING

A wedding is perhaps the most significant worship service many people participate in. A couple stands in the presence of God and friends and makes a covenant that binds the couple together. It's a time for quiet joy and deep feeling.

Clowns at a wedding may seem a bit strange. But when the bride and groom like the idea, clowns can help create a festive mood through a variety of simple and joy-filled moments.

NO LONGER TWO, BUT ONE

Overview—A clown invites the wedding couple to mix two colors of water into one bowl to symbolize "two becoming one."

The Skit* (For one or more clowns)

Gather two clear pitchers and a small, clear punch bowl. Fill the pitchers half-full of water. Put blue food coloring in one pitcher and yellow food coloring in the other. Leave the bowl empty.

Cut three long, narrow felt banners. Using contrasting felt letters, glue the groom's name on one banner and the bride's name on the other. On the third banner, put the two names so they can be distinguished but are intermixed.

---

* Adapted from Floyd Shaffer and Penne Sewall, *Clown Ministry* (Loveland, CO: Group Books, 1984), p. 71. Used by permission.

Attach the groom's banner to the blue-water pitcher, roll it up
and tie it closed. Attach the bride's banner to the yellow-water
pitcher the same way. Attach the third banner to the punch bowl.
Roll it up and tie it with string.

Enter the sanctuary and invite the wedding couple to stand. Hand
the blue-water pitcher to the groom and the yellow-water pitcher to
the bride. Unfurl the banner on each pitcher.

Hold the empty punch bowl so all can see. Then use non-verbal
signs to invite the bride and groom simultaneously to pour their
water into the punch bowl. The water will turn a shade of green.
Then dramatically release the banner on the bowl with the two
names intertwined.

CLOWN SERVANTS

Overview—Clowns are present through the wedding and reception doing various "services," including welcoming guests, decorating the sanctuary and interacting with people at the reception.

The Skit (For one or more clowns)

Instead of performing skits at a wedding, interact with guests to create a festive mood. Here are some ideas:

● Be silent greeters outside the church or chapel. Offer an arm, walk people to the door, open doors with a flourish. Remember, your role is to serve, not to entertain.

● When most people are seated, enter with bunches of helium-filled "love" balloons on strings. Attach them to the ends of every three or four pews. Be sure they're high enough so people can still see the front.

● At the reception, use foot-long pieces of ribbon to tie the bride and groom together by one finger each. Do the same to other couples as it seems appropriate.

WORD TICKLERS

Use these words to spark your own creativity as you adapt these skits—or create your own—for weddings. Add other words you associate with the celebration.

- cake
- flowers
- friends
- gifts
- gowns
- honeymoon
- license
- limousine
- photographs
- reception
- relatives
- rings
- toasts
- tuxedoes
- veil

ALPHABETICAL LIST OF EVENTS